SCIENCE SKILLS 6

T0344172

 **INTERACTION**

1 How much can you remember? Complete the table about the senses.

Sense	Sense organ	Receptors in the ...	Stimulus	Nerve
hearing	ear			
			light	
smell				
				sensory nerves of the peripheral nervous system
		taste buds		

2 Look at the photos and fill in the information.

Sense: _touch_

Sense organ: _skin_

Fact: _Skin is also sensitive to pain, heat and temperature._

Sense: _____

Sense organ: _____

Fact: _____

_____

Sense: _____

Sense organ: _____

Fact: _____

_____

Sense: _____

Sense organ: _____

Fact: _____

_____

3 **Read the article about a blind man. Three sentences are missing from the article. Choose from sentences a-e to fill each gap (1–3). There are two extra sentences.**

Adapting the senses

Bats use echolocation to fly and hunt at night. Due to their poor eyesight, they rely more on their hearing to find their way in the dark. They emit sounds, which reflect off the surfaces of surrounding objects. **(1)** _____ Doing this, bats can determine the location, shape and size of an object and so can Daniel Kish!

Daniel has been blind since he was 13 months old. **(2)** _____ He began making a clicking sound with his tongue and listening to the echo to create images of the world around him. He has even learnt to ride a bike!

Although some people may disapprove of the noise, Daniel continues to click because he knows it is important for blind people to be independent. **(3)** _____ Because of Daniel's bravery, thousands of blind people now have the ability to see, with sound!

a Although they did not have very good hearing.

b As part of an organisation, he now trains many other blind people to use echolocation.

c Sounds cause your eardrums to vibrate, which is transformed into a nerve impulse.

d However, that has never prevented him from moving around on his own.

e When these sounds return to their ears, they notice slight differences in the echo.

4 Circle the odd one out. Write an explanation.

a central nervous system / peripheral nervous system / brain / spinal cord

The peripheral nervous system is the odd one out because the others all belong to the central nervous system.

b peripheral nervous system / sensory neuron / interneuron / motor neuron

_____

c sight / touch / sound / taste

_____

d effector / response / motor neuron / sense organ

_____

e response / receptor / sense organ / sensory neuron

_____

5 How do we respond to a stimulus?
Order the sentences. Write 1–6.

a The brain processes the message's information in the cerebrum. ☐

b The stimulus is changed into an electrical message and passed along the peripheral nervous system. ☐

c A stimulus is detected by receptors in one of our sense organs. 1

d As the control centre, the brain sends out a reaction along motor neurons to an effector. ☐

e A response is carried out by an effector. ☐

f Sensory neurons pass the impulse onto the central nervous system. ☐

6 Are the sentences _true_ or _false_?

a An impulse travels along the axons of neurons.   _____true_____

b We always know when our brain interprets information and coordinates
   a response.   _____

c Reflexes are controlled by our spinal cord, which is a long piece of
   nerve tissue.   _____

d Motor neurons send signals to the brain.   _____

e The nervous system is made up of cells and tissues, but not organs.   _____

**7 Which part of the brain is responsible for these actions?
Match each action to a part of the brain.**

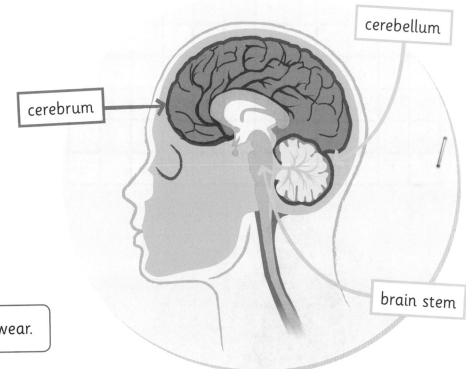

cerebellum

cerebrum

brain stem

a Doing gymnastics.

b Going to sleep.

c Deciding which shirt to wear.

d Running on the football pitch.

g Tasting a delicious ice cream.

e Keeping your heart beating.

h Breathing.

f Remembering your friend's mobile number.

i Feeling sad after doing badly in an exam.

8 How many bones and muscles do you know? Find 22 more words.

r	g	l	u	t	e	u	s	x	q	f	r	m	c	r
s	c	a	p	u	l	a	b	o	w	d	p	j	p	w
s	m	t	r	f	a	c	e	m	u	s	c	l	e	s
f	q	d	t	b	p	e	c	t	o	r	a	l	l	p
i	c	b	q	u	a	d	r	i	c	e	p	s	v	i
b	d	o	r	s	a	l	u	l	n	a	u	l	i	n
u	a	c	l	a	v	i	c	l	e	y	j	r	s	e
l	b	i	c	e	p	s	f	e	m	o	r	i	s	h
a	d	p	j	h	a	b	i	c	e	p	s	b	d	u
k	o	c	a	l	r	q	m	y	c	l	e	s	e	m
h	m	f	v	t	b	t	r	i	c	e	p	s	l	e
d	i	e	r	u	e	p	g	h	i	v	v	l	t	r
b	n	m	t	w	d	l	l	x	r	e	z	r	o	u
w	a	u	s	k	u	l	l	t	i	b	i	a	i	s
h	l	r	a	i	n	z	r	a	d	i	u	s	d	e

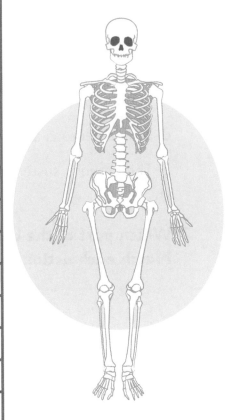

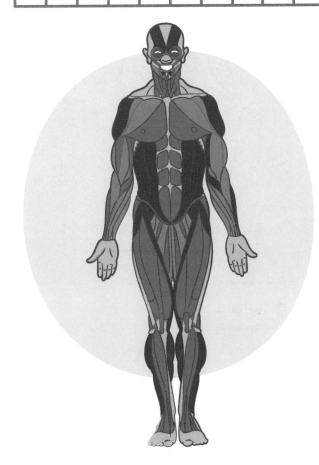

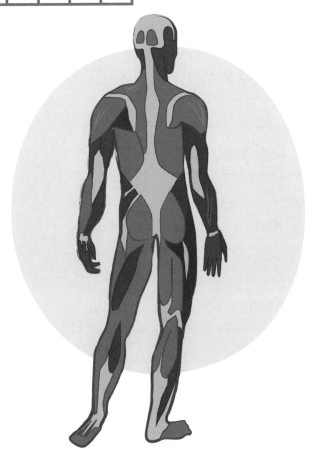

9 Kevin is asking Super Sensational Girl about moving muscles.
Use words from the box to complete the conversation.

bones   contract   muscles   relaxes   shorten

How do our ____muscles____ work
together to move our _____ ?

Well, the brain sends a message to a muscle to
_____ . As muscles do this, they
_____ and move the _____
with them because they are attached.

Why do they say _____ work in pairs?

Because as one muscle contracts, an opposite muscle _____ .

10 Write whether the sentences describe *voluntary* or *involuntary* actions.
Then write whether they are controlled by *skeletal*, *smooth* or *cardiac muscle*.

a Moving our quadriceps muscle to bend our leg.   ___voluntary, skeletal muscle___

b Our heart beating.   _____

c Quickly moving your hand from a hot plate.   _____

d Inhalation and exhalation.   _____

e Moving your arms and legs to swim across a pool.   _____

f Digestion.   _____

11 What is a reflex? Look at the diagram. Then write an explanation
using the words from the box. Write 25–35 words.

impulse   motor neuron   pathway
sensory neuron   spinal cord   stimulus

_____

_____

_____

1 Fill in the diagram with words from the box to show the process of nutrition.

excrete   harmful substances   nutrients
nutrients   oxygen   take in   transform   waste

_____ ➡ _____ ➡ _____

_____   _____   _____

2 Complete the table about nutrients using complete sentences.

Nutrient	Where do I get it?	Why do I need it?
Water	I get water by drinking glasses of it, and from eating fruit and vegetables.	
Oxygen		
Carbohydrates		
Vitamins and minerals		
Proteins		
Fats		

3 Order the sentences to show the process of digestion. Then say where each step takes place.

☐ Food mixes with bile and pancreatic fluid. _____

☐ Water is reabsorbed, and solid waste is expelled out of the body. _____

☐ Gastric juices combine with food. _____

☐ Food mixture is broken down into nutrients and absorbed into the blood. _____

☐ Food is passed from mouth to stomach. _____

☐ Food is crushed into smaller pieces and mixed with saliva. _____

4 Finish the sentences about blood.

a Blood plasma contains mostly _____ .

b Oxygen and carbon dioxide are carried by _____ .

c The function of white blood cells is _____ .

d When you get a cut, platelets _____ .

e Blood's colour _____ .

5 Write *arteries*, *veins* or *both*.

a These are blood vessels. _____

b These carry deoxygenated blood back to the heart. _____

c These connect to capillaries to allow gas exchange. _____

d These transport oxygenated blood around the body. _____

6 Read the description about the circulatory system. Circle the correct words, then label the diagram.

Circulation / Circulatory is the movement of blood, which carries oxygen and nutrients around the body. The heart pumps the blood in two loops.

The first loop is the pulmonary loop. The heart pumps blood to the **body / lungs** where **carbon dioxide / oxygen** is expelled and where **carbon dioxide / oxygen** is picked up. Afterwards, the blood returns to the **body / heart**.

The second loop is the systemic loop. Blood filled with **carbon dioxide / oxygen** is pumped by the heart around the body by the **arteries / veins**. Once the blood reaches the capillaries, the oxygen is expelled, and the blood cells pick up **carbon dioxide / oxygen** and other waste. Then the blood flows back to the heart through the **arteries / veins**.

b _____

c _____

a _____

d _____

e _____

f _____

g _____

7 Match the sentence halves about the respiratory system.

a The respiratory system works …

b The large muscle that controls breathing …

c Gas exchange occurs …

d Air travels from the trachea to …

e Carbon dioxide is expelled …

… is called the diaphragm.

… the bronchi when you inhale.

… together with the circulatory system to deliver oxygen to the body.

… out of the nose and mouth when you exhale.

… in the capillaries.

8 **Place the sentences about inhalation and exhalation in the correct column. Write a–j.**

Inhalation	Exhalation

a Oxygen goes into the lungs.

b The diaphragm rises.

c Oxygen moves into the blood.

d Carbon dioxide flows from the alveoli through bronchioles, bronchi and to the trachea.

e Carbon dioxide moves out of the blood.

f The diaphragm relaxes.

g The diaphragm lowers.

h Oxygen flows from the trachea through bronchi, bronchioles and to the alveoli.

i The diaphragm contracts.

j Carbon dioxide goes out of the lungs.

9 **Label the organs of the excretory system using the words from the box. Then match sentences a–e to the correct places on your drawing.**

bladder   kidney   renal arteries   urethra   ureter

a Urine flows through the urethra and out of our body when we urinate.

b Waste is stored in the bladder.

c Blood passes through the renal arteries.

d Waste is mixed with water and flows down each ureter.

e Blood is filtered through the kidneys.

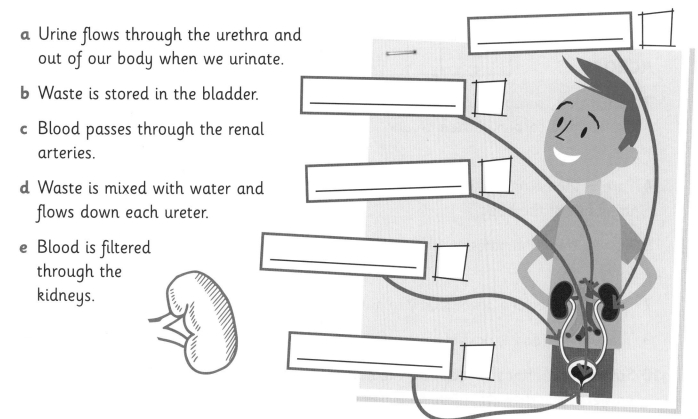

10 Complete the paragraph.

The excretory system has many parts, including our skin. Located in the skin,
(a) _____ excrete **(b)** _____ , a mix of salts and water.
Sweat is excreted through small holes in our skin, called **(c)** _____ .
(d) _____ regulates our body temperature because as the water
(e) _____ , it cools us down.

11 Complete the crossword using words from the unit.

ACROSS

2 Liquid that transports nutrients, oxygen and carbon dioxide around the body.

4 Part of the excretory system that passes urine out of the body.

5 System that eliminates waste and keeps the body cool.

7 Process of breaking down food into nutrients.

9 Tube where food is passed to the stomach.

10 System that brings oxygen into the body and expels carbon dioxide.

DOWN

1 Process with three steps: take in nutrients, transform them, excrete waste.

3 Nutrient carried by red blood cells.

6 Process of blood flowing throughout the body.

8 Muscle that aids in inhaling and exhaling.

12 All these people have got a problem with one of their systems. Match one person to each system.

1 Digestive system ☐

2 Excretory system ☐

3 Circulatory system ☐

4 Respiratory system ☐

a Jennifer:
She is a ballet dancer who is having pain in her feet and hands. Sometimes she cannot feel them.

b Greg:
He is a 32-year-old runner who feels pain when he breathes in after he does a lot of exercise. Sometimes he gets dizzy, too.

c Elizabeth:
She is a 25-year-old swimming instructor who is feeling very tired lately. Normally, she enjoys scuba diving because she can breathe underwater.

d Hannah:
She is a personal trainer who noticed her pulse was very fast after an exercise session. She feels nervous when this happens.

e Joseph:
He is a football player who loves to eat. But lately, he has been having a lot of pain after eating a large meal.

f Cara:
She is a physical education teacher. She frequently has to visit the toilet and has pain when she urinates.

13 Correct the sentences about first aid.

a If a person is bleeding, do not touch the wound.

_____

b When someone has a nosebleed, tip their head backward, then pinch the hard part of their nose.

_____

c If someone is unconscious, do not check their breathing.

_____

d You should always move someone who has a broken bone.

_____

3 WE ARE NATURE

1 How are humans using nature? Write a sentence about each photo.

a _____

b _____

c _____

d _____

e _____

f _____

2 Match each word to its definition. Write 1–4.

a heterotroph

b autotroph

c unicellular

d multicellular

1 An organism that is made up of only one cell.

2 An organism that is made up of more than one cell.

3 An organism that consumes other organisms to get its nutrients.

4 An organism that can produce its own food through photosynthesis.

3 **Read the text and answer the questions. For each question, circle the correct answer *a*, *b*, *c* or *d*.**

Extremophiles

Can you imagine living at the bottom of the ocean or at the top of Mount Everest? The organisms that call hydrothermal vents, ice packs and even toxic waste home are properly named extremophiles!

Extremophiles are found in all five kingdoms, though most are microorganisms. These creatures survive in the most intense habitats: under high pressure, in extremely hot or cold temperatures, in salt, acid or alkaline, and without oxygen. One archaic bacterium grows at 122°C, the highest recorded on Earth!

Studying species from extreme environments has applications when searching for life beyond Earth. Extremophiles are considered model organisms for extra-terrestrial life. The organisms found in the *Rio Tinto*, for instance, may be similar to potential living things on Mars.

Not only do extremophiles tell us about the range of conditions that make life possible, scientists are also investigating their use for biofuels, medicines, chemicals, and even lactose-free milk! For example, metal-loving species are able to remove metals from the soil, which prevents water pollution. Therefore, extremophiles may help us save the environment!

1 Which organism could not be an extremophile?

  a a protist   **c** a human

  b a fungus   **d** a plant

2 Some extremophiles live ...

  a without light.   **c** in your classroom.

  b on the moon.   **d** in milk.

3 Why are extremophiles useful for scientists to study?

  a Because they need medicine.

  b Because they are so small.

  c Because they can easily adapt to all environments.

  d Because they survive conditions similar to other places in the universe.

4 What would be a good introduction to this article?

  a | Extremophiles live in all places in our Solar System.

  b | In this article, a scientist explains why extremophiles are useful.

  c | Understanding extreme environments is important for people who are allergic to lactose.

  d | If you want to know how organisms survive in the ocean, then read this article.

4 Write definitions for the following words. Give two examples of each.

 a Omnivore: _____

 _____

 b Carnivore: _____

 _____

 c Herbivore: _____

 _____

5 Answer the questions about the five kingdoms.

 a Which kingdoms are autotrophs?

 _____

 _____

 b In which kingdoms do the organisms reproduce sexually?

 _____

 c In which kingdoms are the organisms unicellular?

 _____

 d List two subgroups of the plant and animal kingdoms.

 Plant kingdom: _____

 Animal kingdom: _____

6 Circle the odd one out, then write which kingdom the other organisms belong to.

 a octopus / swan / butterfly / oak tree   _____

 b rose / mushroom / grass / oak tree   _____

 c mushroom / yeast / bacteria / mould   _____

 d yeast / seaweed / alga / protozoan   _____

 e Which kingdom is missing?   _____

7 Label the diagram of photosynthesis with the words and phrases from the box.

carbon dioxide   carbon dioxide enters leaf through stomata
glucose   light energy   oxygen   sugar leaves leaf
water and minerals   water enters leaf

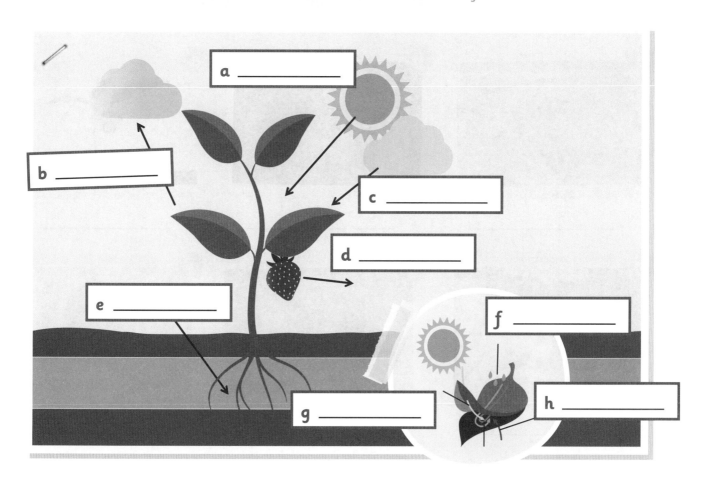

a _____

b _____

c _____

d _____

e _____

f _____

g _____

h _____

**8 How do plants use sunlight to make their own food?
Order the sentences. Write 1–5.**

a Water and minerals reach the plant's leaves,
carbon dioxide enters through stomata, and light
energy is absorbed by chlorophyll.

b Water and minerals move up the xylem in the plant's stem.

c Oxygen is released into the air, while the phloem transports the
glucose to other parts of the plant.

d The roots of a plant take up water and minerals from the soil.

e Light energy is used to combine carbon dioxide with water and minerals.

9 **How do these organisms use water? For each organism, write 1–6.**

1 As a habitat   **4** To move around the environment

2 To transport molecules   **5** To make energy

3 For bodily functions   **6** To absorb food

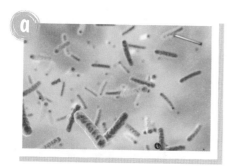

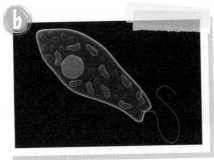

_____   _____   _____

_____   _____   _____

10 **In what other ways do humans use water?**
Make a list.

-
-
-
-
-
-
-
-
-
-

11 Are the sentences about water *true* or *false*?

a Water is an unlimited resource. _____

b Humans transform rivers for
drinking water and electricity. _____

c Humans never affect the aquatic habitats of other organisms. _____

d The water from your kitchen tap can come from groundwater. _____

e Salt water is not useful. _____

f Cleaning polluted water is easy and cheap. _____

12 Who is protecting the environment? Tick the boxes.

a Trees are cut down for farmland. ☐   Trees are planted. ☑

b A boy throws rubbish in the bin. ☐   A boy throws rubbish on the ground. ☐

c A company mines for gold, coal or oil. ☐   Products are recycled and ores reused. ☐

d Waste water flows into a river. ☐   Waste water is treated. ☐

e A farm collects and treats its runoff. ☐   A farm produces agricultural runoff. ☐

f A city grows without control. ☐   A city develops sustainably. ☐

13 Complete the sentences using the words on the right.

a _____ eliminates many
organisms' habitats by cutting down too many trees.

agricultural runoff

b A _____ is an organism that
shows us when an ecosystem is unbalanced.

bioindicator

c Through _____ , it is
possible to restore ecological equilibrium by sharing land
space with other living things.

deforestation

d Chemicals and toxins from farms, called
_____ , pollute river water.

land management

e Although we need wood as a resource, it is still important to
protect _____ .

natural forests

4 MIXTURES

1 **Draw how molecules look in the solid, liquid and gaseous states of matter. Then match the sentences to the correct state of matter.**

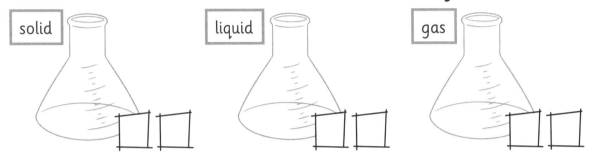

solid | liquid | gas

a Molecules in this state have the most energy.

b Molecules in this state have the least energy.

c Molecules in this state have a medium amount of energy.

d Molecules in this state take the shape of their container.

e Molecules in this state move around and completely fill their container.

f Molecules in this state remain close together and do not move around very much.

2 **Complete the sentences. Give an example of each.**

a _____ is when a liquid is transformed into a gas.

For example: _____

b When a _____ changes directly into a gas, sublimation occurs.

For example: _____

c We can see a liquid changing into a _____ during solidification.

For example: _____

d _____ is when a gas turns into a liquid.

For example: _____

e When lots of energy is added, a solid is transformed into a _____ ,
which is a process called melting.

For example: _____

3 Complete the chart with words and drawings.

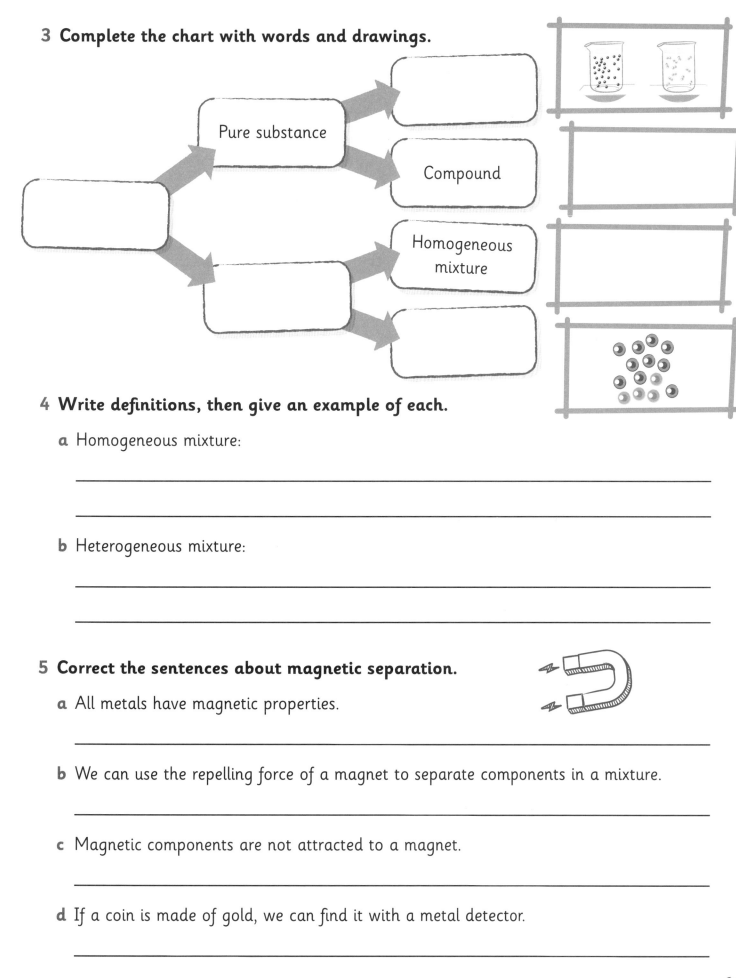

Pure substance

Compound

Homogeneous mixture

4 Write definitions, then give an example of each.

a Homogeneous mixture:

_____

_____

b Heterogeneous mixture:

_____

_____

5 Correct the sentences about magnetic separation.

a All metals have magnetic properties.

_____

b We can use the repelling force of a magnet to separate components in a mixture.

_____

c Magnetic components are not attracted to a magnet.

_____

d If a coin is made of gold, we can find it with a metal detector.

_____

6 Complete the sentences about filtration.

a Filtration allows us to separate an _____ solid from a liquid.

b An insoluble substance will never _____ in a solvent.

c By using a _____ with small holes, we can separate the components of a mixture.

d Separation using _____ is based on size of the molecules. Small molecules can pass through a filter, while larger molecules do not.

e Filters should allow _____ to pass through, but trap _____ .

f We call the component of the mixture that is trapped in the filter the _____ .

g The component of the mixture that passes through the filter is called the _____ .

7 Describe what is happening in the picture. Use words from the box to help you.

boil evaporate heat soluble

_____

_____

_____

_____

8 How can we use distillation to separate a mixture?
Order the sentences. Write 1–5.

   a The gas passes through a cooling chamber where it condenses. ☐

   b Each of the components boil at different temperatures. Component 1 of the mixture boils first, at a lower temperature. ☐

   c The condensed component is collected in a separate container, while the other component remains in the original container. ☐

   d The evaporated component is now in a gaseous state and rises. ☐

   e Heat the liquid mixture so that it boils. ☐

9 Write an advantage and a disadvantage of each method of separation.

	Advantage	Disadvantage

10 Write the word that belongs to each definition. Then find it in the word search below.

a What makes up everything around us. _____

b Each substance in a mixture. _____

c Two or more atoms joined together. _____

d The substance that dissolves in a liquid. _____

e A substance that contains all the same atom or molecule. _____

f The smallest particle that makes up matter. _____

g A substance that will not dissolve in a liquid. _____

h Two or more substances that are combined but can be physically separated.

_____

i A molecule made up of only one type of atom. _____

j A liquid that dissolves a soluble component. _____

m	m	d	j	w	a	b	r	o	v	p	u	o	l	x
i	e	r	b	x	p	c	j	t	e	e	c	e	k	d
f	c	y	g	j	c	n	o	n	m	r	w	p	e	g
q	m	j	w	u	o	m	g	m	l	c	y	u	e	g
s	w	e	b	k	m	n	m	o	p	n	b	r	a	f
o	i	s	g	g	p	t	i	l	s	o	q	e	q	f
l	n	o	g	f	o	u	x	e	f	u	u	c	c	r
v	s	l	l	m	n	q	t	c	r	c	u	n	p	v
e	o	u	x	a	e	j	u	u	a	v	e	u	d	s
n	l	t	m	t	n	m	r	l	t	e	c	t	t	x
t	u	e	y	t	t	h	e	e	o	s	q	q	l	m
t	b	i	s	e	i	r	d	i	m	s	q	n	h	j
x	l	s	c	r	g	n	f	y	n	w	g	n	o	a
e	e	v	e	l	e	m	e	n	t	h	b	u	b	x
c	o	z	d	g	l	n	s	p	u	y	d	z	u	v

11 Complete the table about separating mixtures.

Method	Component 1	Component 2	Process
Paper chromatography	Soluble solid	Liquid	Use a vertical paper filter to separate both components.
Magnetic Separation			
Filtration			
Evaporation			
Distillation			

12 A scientist's laboratory journal has become mixed up! Help him sort it by identifying which form of separation is being described.

1 It is extremely important to keep both components of the liquid mixture.

    a Evaporation
    b Distillation
    c Magnetic separation

2 Today I was testing certain metals that are magnetic. I've discovered that I can use a detector to separate iron from gold.

    a Evaporation
    b Distillation
    c Magnetic separation

3 Dear Dr Smith, we only need the salt from the mixture. Don't worry about the water at all!

    a Filtration
    b Evaporation
    c Distillation

4 Remember, it is easy to use special paper with tiny holes when you separate an insoluble solid from a liquid.

    a Filtration
    b Evaporation
    c Distillation

5 CHEMICAL REACTIONS

1 Circle the correct word to complete the text.

In a **(a)** *physical* / *chemical* reaction, the original substances, called
(b) *reactants* / *products*, are transformed into new substances called
(c) *reactants* / *products*. As the reaction occurs, the **(d)** *original* / *final*
properties of the **(e)** *reactants* / *products* completely change. Chemical reactions
can be caused by **(f)** *sound* / *thermal* energy, oxygen, bacteria or fungi.

2 Read the text and answer the questions.

Mary and her brother, John, want to make a pizza.
They find lots of ingredients in the cupboard, as well
as a recipe book. John reads out the recipe and tells
Mary to mix warm water and yeast in one bowl for
five minutes. In another bowl, John combines flour,
sugar and salt. Afterwards, they mix the ingredients
from both bowls together, and then add oil. They
leave the mixture to rise in a warm place for one hour.
Once it has risen, they knead the dough and roll it
out in a circle. They place it in the oven to bake for
20 minutes and enjoy delicious pizza afterwards!

a How many chemical reactions are taking place?

_____

b What are the original reactants?

_____

c How do the reactants change after the reaction?

_____

d What are the products?

_____

3 Compare mixtures to chemical reactions. Write a–e in the table.

Mixtures	Chemical reactions	Both

a Two or more substances combined.

b After combining, the substances maintain original properties.

c After combining, the substances' original properties change.

d Products are now chemically linked.

e Components can be easily separated because they are not chemically linked.

4 Match the characteristics of chemical reactions to their definitions.

Gas formation ☐

Colour change ☐

Energy change ☐

Precipitate formation ☐

a When the product of the reaction gets warmer, colder or produces light.

b When one of the products of the reaction is in a gaseous state or emits a different smell.

c When the product of the reaction is a different colour to the reactants.

d When one of the products of the reaction becomes a solid.

5 Prove it's a chemical reaction! Read the descriptions. Which characteristics prove that a chemical reaction is taking place?

a A metal screwdriver is left outside in the rain. After a few days, it turns reddish brown.

_____

b Pupils in a science class mix sodium bicarbonate (white solid) and vinegar (clear liquid). They use the foam and bubbles that are produced to demonstrate a volcano.

_____

c As two clear liquids are mixed together, scientists notice a white solid forming at the bottom of the container. After a few minutes, the outside of the container feels colder.

_____

d Two clear liquids are mixed to produce a red liquid that smells like almonds.

_____

6 Label and explain the diagram. Use words from the box to help you.

air   ash   energy   fire   fuel   heat   light   oxygen   smoke   wood

a _____

_____

b _____

_____

c _____

_____

7 Read the text below and think of the word that best fits each gap. Use one word in each gap.

Forest Fires

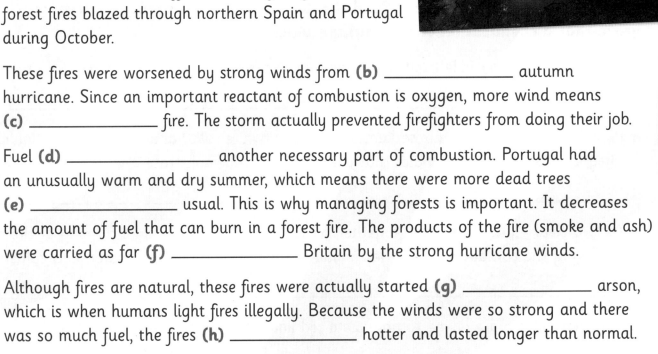

As our climate gets warmer, we are beginning to see **(a)** _____ effects in many ways. In 2017, forest fires blazed through northern Spain and Portugal during October.

These fires were worsened by strong winds from **(b)** _____ autumn hurricane. Since an important reactant of combustion is oxygen, more wind means **(c)** _____ fire. The storm actually prevented firefighters from doing their job.

Fuel **(d)** _____ another necessary part of combustion. Portugal had an unusually warm and dry summer, which means there were more dead trees **(e)** _____ usual. This is why managing forests is important. It decreases the amount of fuel that can burn in a forest fire. The products of the fire (smoke and ash) were carried as far **(f)** _____ Britain by the strong hurricane winds.

Although fires are natural, these fires were actually started **(g)** _____ arson, which is when humans light fires illegally. Because the winds were so strong and there was so much fuel, the fires **(h)** _____ hotter and lasted longer than normal.

8 **Answer the questions.**

a What is oxidation?

_____

_____

b How does it affect these substances? Give examples.

Metal: _____

Food: _____

9 **Circle the substances that are a result of fermentation.**

pizza crust   iron   ham   bread   fruit

yeast   sugar   salami   lactic acid

sauerkraut   yoghurt   cheese   metal

10 **Which reaction is taking place in each photo? Write _combustion_, _oxidation_ or _fermentation_. Write the reactants and the products for each one.**

a

_____

_____

b

_____

_____

c

_____

_____

d

_____

_____

e

_____

_____

f

_____

_____

11 Complete the crossword using words from the unit.

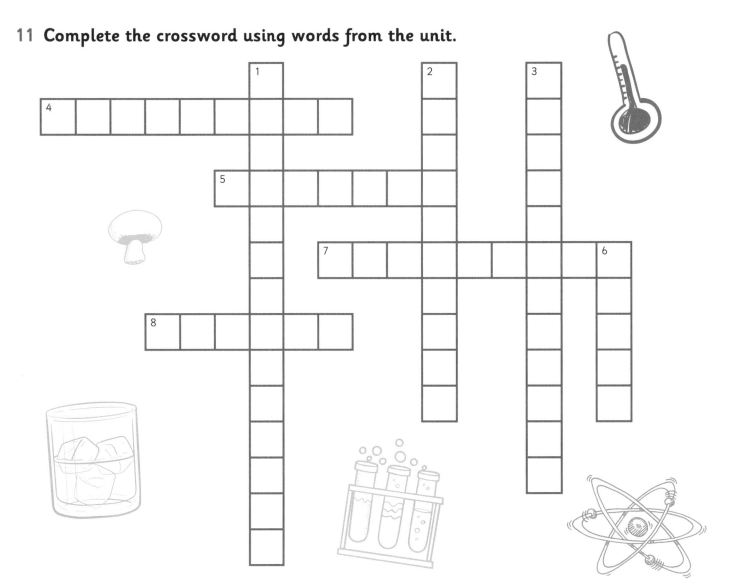

DOWN

1 Living things that cause fermentation.

2 One of the products that bacteria produce during fermentation.

3 The transformation of sugars into organic substances by bacteria and fungi.

6 The reactant that bacteria and fungi transform into organic substances.

ACROSS

4 A chemical reaction where a substance gains oxygen.

5 A component that results from a chemical reaction.

7 The components with original properties that take part in a chemical reaction.

8 A gas that makes up 21% of the air we breathe.

12 Decide if the sentences describe combustion, oxidation or fermentation. Write C, O or F. You can write more than one letter if necessary.

a It reacts with oxygen to produce a new substance. _____

b It breaks down the original reactants to form a new substance. _____

c It is a chemical reaction. _____

d It is caused by microorganisms. _____

e It forms new products as the reaction occurs. _____

f It requires energy to occur. _____

g It produces light, heat, ash and smoke as products. _____

h It affects food. _____

i It affects metals. _____

j When oxygen reacts with water to produce rust. _____

k It occurs naturally in nature. _____

l It occurs when no oxygen is present. _____

13 Are chemical reactions useful? Complete the chart.

Reaction	Advantage	Disadvantage

6 **MAGNETISM**

1 **Look at the following materials. Tick the ones that are magnetic and then explain what this means.**

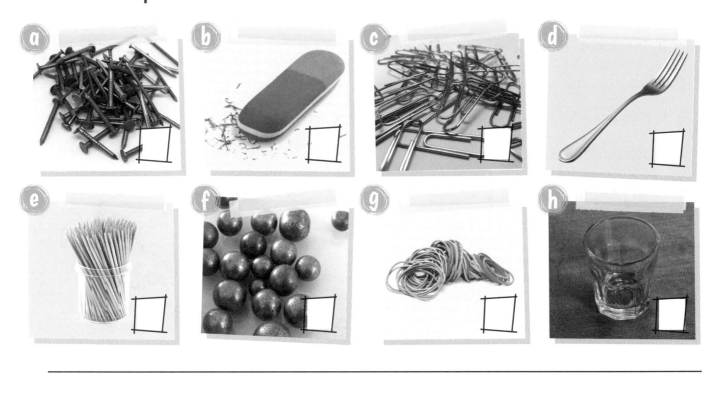

a☐ b☐ c☐ d☐

e☐ f☐ g☐ h☐

_____

_____

_____

2 **You have been given a bar magnet and some iron filings. Draw what you would see if you placed the iron filings around the magnet.**

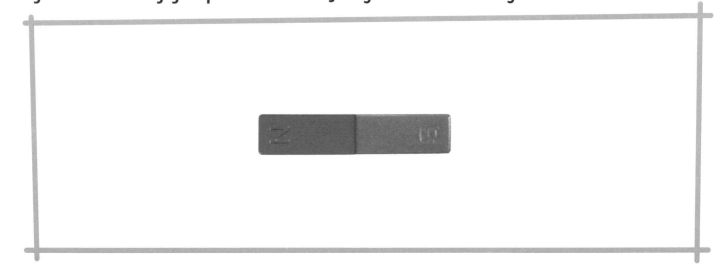

3 **Look at the pictures and label the poles. Explain how each set of magnets react in each case.**

a _____

_____

_____

b _____

_____

_____

4 **Read the texts and explain what you would do in each case.**

a

In the laboratory, your science teacher gives you and your partner three metal rods: one made of aluminium, one made of iron, and one magnet. She says that you must perform an experiment.

_____

_____

b

As you are walking home from school, something shiny on the ground catches your eye. When you look down you see a piece of metal on the pavement, so you pick it up and take it home. You are not sure whether or not it is jewellery, but it looks like it. You want to see if it is worth money.

_____

_____

c

At breaktime, your friend shows you two metal rods. He tells you one is a magnet and one is not. He will give you his bag of delicious sweets if you can figure out which one is the magnet using only the rods. (Hint: The centre of a true magnet has a very weak magnetic field.)

_____

_____

5 **Label the diagram with the words from the box. Answer the questions.**

magnetic
geographical   field
North   South
Pole   iron   core

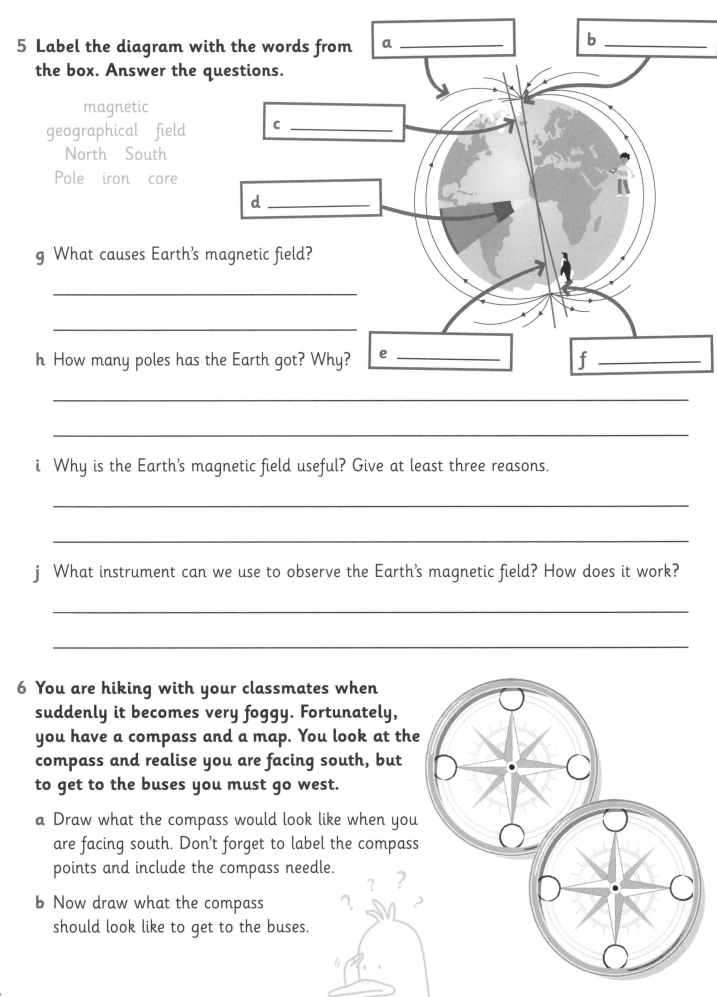

a _____

b _____

c _____

d _____

e _____

f _____

g What causes Earth's magnetic field?

_____

_____

h How many poles has the Earth got? Why?

_____

_____

i Why is the Earth's magnetic field useful? Give at least three reasons.

_____

_____

j What instrument can we use to observe the Earth's magnetic field? How does it work?

_____

_____

6 **You are hiking with your classmates when suddenly it becomes very foggy. Fortunately, you have a compass and a map. You look at the compass and realise you are facing south, but to get to the buses you must go west.**

a Draw what the compass would look like when you are facing south. Don't forget to label the compass points and include the compass needle.

b Now draw what the compass should look like to get to the buses.

7 Label the diagrams to demonstrate how an electromagnet works.

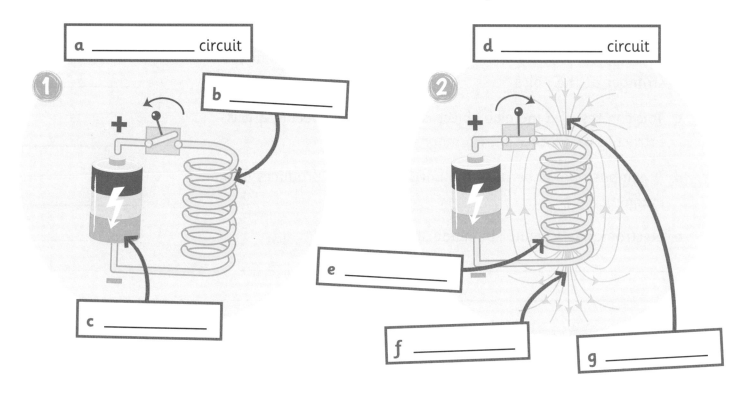

a _____ circuit

b _____

c _____

d _____ circuit

e _____

f _____

g _____

How is illustration **2** different from illustration **1**? Why?

_____

_____

_____

8 Explain how an electric doorbell works. Order the sentences by writing the numbers 1–6.

a The electromagnet turns off and the metal arm moves back to its original place. ☐

b The electromagnet attracts a metal arm whose movement makes a sound. ☐

c Someone presses the doorbell, which closes an electric circuit. ☐

d The metal arm moves out of position, so the circuit is now open. ☐

e The circuit is now back in its original state. ☐

f Electric current is able to flow through the circuit, and the electromagnet in the doorbell makes a magnetic field. ☐

9 Are the sentences *true* or *false*? Correct the false sentences.

a All metals are magnetic. _____

b All magnets produce a magnetic field with field lines that are stronger at the poles. _____

c You can test if a metallic object is a magnet by seeing if it is attracted to another known magnet. _____

d A compass works because the Earth's iron core produces a giant magnetic field. _____

e Electromagnets cannot be made stronger. _____

_____

_____

_____

10 Circle the odd one out and explain why it is different.

a paper clip / rubber band / fork / scissors

_____

b cobalt / nickel / gold / iron

_____

c magnetite / nickel / cobalt / iron

_____

d loudspeakers / hairdryer / doorbell / compass

_____

11 Complete the sentences to describe the different types of magnets.

a Permanent magnets …

_____

b Temporary magnets …

_____

c Electromagnets …

_____

12 Read the text below and choose the correct word for each space. For each question, circle the correct word.

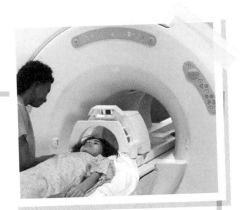

Magnets in Medicine

A magnetic resonance imaging (MRI) scanner is a machine that uses strong magnetic fields and radio waves to produce detailed images of the **(a)** ….. of the body.

During the scan, you lie inside **(b)** ….. large tube that contains powerful magnets. Because your body is made up **(c)** ….. water, the magnets cause the hydrogen protons in your body, which act like tiny magnets, to line up in the same direction. This is similar to how a needle is attracted to a magnet in a compass.

The machine sends radio waves through the body, knocking the hydrogen protons out of order. When the radio waves are turned off, the protons straighten out. We can find the exact location of these protons **(d)** ….. signals that form pictures on a screen.

Unlike X-rays, MRIs can examine almost any part of the body, including your brain, heart and all your **(e)** ….. organs. The results help doctors understand their patients' problems and help them plan treatments. Plus, it's **(f)** ….. and painless, even a baby can have an MRI scan!

a internal / inside / exterior / outside

b their / they're / it's / a

c of / off / with / to

d use / used / using / uses

e changed / special / various / different

f safe / safety / secure / healthy

HOW DO YOU SAY ... ?

Unit 1: Interaction

English	Your language
axon (n)	_____
cardiac (adj)	_____
cartilage (n)	_____
contract (v)	_____
dendrite (n)	_____
effector (n)	_____
flexible (adj)	_____
impulse (n)	_____
interact (v)	_____
involuntary (adj)	_____
joint (n)	_____
musculoskeletal system (n)	_____
neuron (n)	_____
receptor (n)	_____
reflex (n)	_____
relax (v)	_____
response (n)	_____
sense organ (n)	_____
stimulus (n)	_____
skeletal (adj)	_____
smooth (adj)	_____

Unit 2: Nutrition

English	Your language
absorption (n)	_____
airway (n)	_____
bile (n)	_____
blood vessel (n)	_____
carbon dioxide (n)	_____
circulation (n)	_____
diet (n)	_____
digestion (n)	_____
energy (n)	_____
excrete (v)	_____
gastric juice (n)	_____
heterotroph (n)	_____
nutrient (n)	_____
nutrition (n)	_____
oesophagus (n)	_____
oxygen (n)	_____
pancreas (n)	_____
respiration (n)	_____
saliva (n)	_____
take in (v)	_____
transform (v)	_____
vaccine (n)	_____

Unit 3: We are nature		Unit 4: Mixtures	
English	Your language	English	Your language
adaptable (adj)	_____	atom (n)	_____
autotroph (n)	_____	component (n)	_____
chlorophyll (n)	_____	condensation (n)	_____
environment (n)	_____	dissolved (adj)	_____
flowering (adj)	_____	distillation (n)	_____
glucose (n)	_____	element (n)	_____
groundwater (n)	_____	evaporation (n)	_____
heterotroph (n)	_____	filter (n)	_____
instrument (n)	_____	filtration (n)	_____
invertebrate (n)	_____	filtrate (n)	_____
kingdom (n)	_____	heterogeneous (adj)	_____
microscope (n)	_____	homogeneous (adj)	_____
non-flowering (adj)	_____	insoluble (adj)	_____
non-vascular (adj)	_____	matter (n)	_____
phloem (n)	_____	molecule (n)	_____
photosynthesis (n)	_____	property (n)	_____
producer (n)	_____	pure substance (n)	_____
resource (n)	_____	residue (n)	_____
runoff (n)	_____	separation (n)	_____
sewage treatment (n)	_____	solidification (n)	_____
stomata (n)	_____	solute (n)	_____
vertebrate (n)	_____	solvent (n)	_____
vascular (adj)	_____	state of matter (n)	_____
xylem (n)	_____	sublimation (n)	_____

Unit 5: Chemical reactions

English	Your language
ash (n)	_____
bacteria (n)	_____
carbon dioxide (n)	_____
chemical bond (n)	_____
combustion (n)	_____
endothermic (adj)	_____
exothermic (adj)	_____
fermentation (n)	_____
fire (n)	_____
food preservation (n)	_____
fuel (n)	_____
fungi (n)	_____
lactic acid (n)	_____
microorganism (n)	_____
oxidation (n)	_____
precipitate (n)	_____
product (n)	_____
reactant (n)	_____
rust (n)	_____
smoke (n)	_____
sugar (n)	_____

Unit 6: Magnetism

English	Your language
attract (v)	_____
compass (n)	_____
compass rose (n)	_____
electricity (n)	_____
electric current (n)	_____
electromagnet (n)	_____
electromagnetism (n)	_____
field line (n)	_____
induced (adj)	_____
iron (n)	_____
magnet (n)	_____
magnetic field (n)	_____
magnetic pole (n)	_____
magnetised (adj)	_____
magnetism (n)	_____
magnetite (n)	_____
man-made (adj)	_____
North Pole (n)	_____
permanent (adj)	_____
repel (v)	_____
solar wind (n)	_____
South Pole (n)	_____